TECHNOLOGY HOW INFLUENCES ORGANIZATIONAL RESOURCE CHANGES

JOHN LOK

Contents

Preface

Introduction

Any organizations must need resources to be provided in order to supply for their organizational development. However, resouces may include human resources, equipment facilities resources , earth natural resource e.g. land, water wood, gas et. building material resources, even working time resources , technological etc. different kinds of resources. Thus, it seems that any organizations must need some resources to help their organizational daily operation in success.

The question concerns what the best resources used strategies to be achieve the most efficiency or the best performance to be organizational development.

In my these series, I shall explain what factors may influence an organizations to use that resources in the most efficient effectiveness in order to avoid to waste nature or human or material resources . Readers can learn what the strategies may be applied to avoid organizational wasting resource behaviors. In my this book four series, I shall apply how and why organization resource shortage can bring what influence to organizational and social change.

How can business apply right or reasonable science management principle to manage that businesses effectively and efficiently in order to achieve sale and profit raising aim in the least resource suitation? Otherwise, applying wrong or unreasonable science management principle , it can bring what disadvantages or negative impacts to the businesses. IN my this chapter, I shall attempt to indicate above questions . Readers can have more clear view whether why the kinds of science resource management methods are not suitable to be applied to the kind of organizations to bring negative impact consequences.

Prologue

Tablof content

Chapter 1

Internet will be intangible technology knowledge resource to e-commerce organization

Chapter 2

Organization efficient using resources economic method

Chapter 3

The relationship between resource shortage and consumer behavior

Can bring either positive or negative or both impact to change consumer behavior when the consumer begins to feel resource shrtage occurrence to choose to buy the kind of product or consume the kind of service?

How does a consumer make choice with scarce resources?

Do they have relationship between organizational technology resource economic behavior and social needs?

Why have they interaction to influence resource supply between orgaizations and societies?

Chapter 4

Ecommerce organization resource management strategy

How an ecommerce organization resource affects ssociety?

Why has online webstore's information technology resource close relationship to influence online buyers number and social job chance?

How do organizational resources affect organizational change?

How to build organizatonal resource using right psychology

changed ?
Reasons why human behavior may influence economic recession or growth
?
How employee behavior influences organizational development?
Artificial intelligent Human clever and art creating ability methods
Why does technology raise online products sale demand and reduces shops products sale demand?
Does car technological development reach mature stage to help economic development?
Investing in office technology can bring what advantages

Internet will be intangible technology knowledge resource to e-commerce organization

What are organizational resources ? What do organizational resources mean? What kinds of organizational resources are needed? What negative impact may be influenced if organizations lack enough resources to influence organizational development? Does working time belong to organizational time resources to influence employee individual efficiency e.g. how arranging enough employee to do the identified task in the most short time in order to achieve the most efficient performane? I shall attempt to identify examples to explain above questions as below:

In general, organizational resources are all assets, that are available to a firm for use during the production process. The four basic types of organizational resources are human, monetary , raw materials and capital. Organizational resources are combined, used and transofrmed to finished products during the production process. For organizational human resource example, human resource activities full under the following five core functions: staffing, development, compensation, safety and health core functions.

● HR resource

HR conducts a wide variety of activities. However, in any organizations, the major resources used by organizations are often described as follow (1) human resources (2) financial respirces (3) physical resources and (4) information resources. Managers are responsible for acquring and managing the resources to accomplosh goals. Hence, in organizational HR aspect, it may include these function, such as retirement and selection, performance management , learning and development, succession planning, compensation and benefits, human resource information systems. Because considering that for many organizations employees themselves represent a significant cost to the business, if the organization can use its employees in efficiency.

Then, it can avoid human resource in excess or in surplus on wasting challenge. Then , its employee cost or salary can be reduced. I t means that it does not need to employ in excess employees number, but the organization can still achieve itself the most efficient performance. Hence, any organizations must need to learn how to avoid " in excess employees number supply or wasting employee working behaviors" challenge . Because if some tasks do not need many employees to work together, it can still be achieved efficiency . Then , the organization ought not employee too many or excess employees to finish the kind of task. Thus, learning how to use efficient human resources, it can help organizations to avoid wasting working time to any departments employees. For example, when one factory has limited land to be supplied to become warehouse in order to help it to keep sticks. If it has excess logistic or factory workers number. Then, they are wasting working time to do not important tasks in warehouse, it means that if the factory has only one warehouse, but its area is small, it can allow maximum 50 workers to stay in the warehouse , but the warehouse has above 100 workers are staying to deliver goods in the small warehouse . Then, they must not actieve the most efficiency , even their delivery or transport goods performance will be influenced to worse by noise and crowd warehouse working environment. Hence, excess employees number in any working environment, which can not improve organizational performance or riase efficiency any organizations can not neglect " excess employees number" organizatinal HR resource arranging issue.

The solution concerns arranging the most right or the most exact empllyees number in order to supply to any organizational departments. Then, the organization can avoid wasting employee individual talent, reducing employing cost, improvig performance, achieving the most efficiency. Resource capacity means resource pool who are available in the organization to take up to appropriate human resource arrangement to assist any departmental development in long term efficiency. Hence, organizational human rsources may become talent tangible assets or foolish tangible assets. It depends on how the organization's resource capacity tasks arrangement to every employee in different departments. If the organization neglects how to arrange every employee task in the most exact or the most appropriate employees number in the department.

The department's efficiency must be caused worse, because excess employees number, it can not help it to achieve the most efficiency aim, even it may influence the excess employees , themselves feel waste working hours to do the not essential or not important tasks. Then, the organization may cause talent employee to become foolish employee. Otherwise, the organization's efficiency to be worse, because when the department has not enough employees to work. Then , any one employee may feel hard to work, his/her emotion may be influenced to negative, then his/her workig behavior may b inefficiency or lazy working. On consequence, the organization may bring economic loss, due to employee individual lasy working behavior, negative working emotion, even high working pressure may be caused, when one employee needs to do more , then the employee's task, but his/her salary can not increase. He/she will feel unfair to compare the another department employee, he /she does not need to spend long working hours or overtime to work per day. SO, any organization needs to avoid shortage employee supply or excess employee supply issue to any departments. Appropriare employees number is the best strategy in order to raise overall organizational efficiency.

● Time resource

Instead of human resource, land, raw material, earth natural resource, electricity, gas may be organization resources . Whether time may be organizational resources, organizational time management vires time as a scarce resource that must be invested as effectivity. Time is an infinite resource . If not properly managed on in an organization. It can have a negative impact on both employer's and employee's productivity. So, organizations should ensure that workers are well equipped to manage time in their duties.So, in management view, any organization managers must need to consider how to manage time, eg . how to arrange employees to work in different departments in order to achieve the most efficiency. They need to understand which resources are in short supply and focus on the prioritizing work across shared resources, they need agree on a common approach, they also need to realize resource management is an ongoing process. Thus, time is an often ignored but invaluable resource in any organization. All activities be it procurement.

An organization's time, in contrast, goes largely unmanaged. Although, phone calls, email, instant messages , meetings, they are general daily tasks to any organizations managers, but mangers need to know how to arrange the most urgent tasks in prior. For example, if the manager can not arrange a meeting to the discuss client tomorroe, as well as the manager needs to spend two hours to meeting with overall 200 employees to discuss how to solve improving efficiency challenge tomorroe. So, this manager needs to make choice whether he ought spend two hours meeting to the business client, or two hours meeting to 200 employees. If he chooses to meet the business client tomorrow, he will help his firm to win the important business chance, but he can not discuss how to improve efficiency in order to find the best method to let 200 employees to know tomorrow. Thus, tomorrow time management will be one importat time resource to the manager. The manager needs to arrange tomorrow two hours time how to plan business meting or efficiency imporvement meerting either to his 200 employees or the one business client. Because if the manager decided to meet the client, he must need to spend today time to aplan or organize how to arrange either business proposal content for the business client or organizational operational challenge questions and solutions for his 200 employees . So, today time management is also important time resource to influence tomorrow either the success business meeting or the organizational 200 employees meeting. So, it seems that time management may be one important resource to any managers more than general employees in any organizations.

If the manager can know how to manager his/her time to do any prior tasks, then he/she may help the organization to raise efficiency or improve performance. Otherwise, if the manager can not know how arrange what prior urgent task needs to be finished. Then, worse performance or inefficiency may be influenced to cause. So, if the organization manager can know how to make time arrangement, I believe that he can help the organization employees to raise efficiency more easily.

New economy brings new way of resource management. The old loyalty and job security -based organization changes, organizations know that the assets are largely made up employees (HRM), but many new organizations begin to believe technology is important assets, such as Amazon is global ecommerce delivery service organization. It seems internet high technology is its important intangible resource to help it earn global e-buyers number increases . So , many organizations began to believe that technology will be important resource, such as internet can provide online business chance. With all the businesses are taking full advantage of internet, for example, the US department estimates that the value of retail e-commerce in 2000 year was about $25 billion, which represents less than 1% of US retail sales. Despite this, interest in e-business remains high.

● Why internet may be main technology resource to organizations?

E-commere needs strategy in order to win competitors, questions include: What criteria do customers use to choose between our firms and competitors? How do the best employees decision whether to join? What business environment attracts and keeps the best suppliers making with our firms? What characteristics draw the most royal invesdtors to our firms? e.g. Amazon . com's web site and Wal-mart's can apply internet technology resource to create each e-store to let e-buyers to choose any kinds of products to buy athome conveniently. Hence, internet technology, even future other kinds of new technology may be main technology resources to organizations, when they can help organizations to raise sale competitive effort.

I mean that digital economy will be one kind new digital resource to future any organizations. The essential piece is the knowledge, it is what give it life and what makes it an interesting and fulifulling purchase and sale channel for people to spend their time , such as e-commerce virtual organization may be leaded to let purchase and ale transactions carry on easily from online websites. Hence, internet may be main knowledge management (intellectual capital) resource to any e-commerce organizations. It is about the storage, transfer knowledge.

For Amazon publish example, e-books will be knowledge as an object, like a book in library. Amazon can apply internet technology to help it to sell any author's ebooks from its book estores. So, ebooks are Amazon's knowledge resources to help it to create readers incomes. E-books is intangible knowledge resource to Amazon . Any authors' paper and ebooks will be sold cheap price to help Amazon to attract global readers to choose to buy its ebooks from its different countries e-webstores at home conveniently.

Hence, any e-commerce organizations also need HRM (emanagers) to help them to deliver a superior value (world class capabilities) in both te virtual and physical world. E-management will be another main human resources to e-commerce organizations. Why does e-management will be future main

HRM resource to e-commerce organization? The reasons may include:
E-management demands in sort of managerial/e-commerce sale strategy effort, skills at positioning the firm within a networm of industries, e-management also demands the ability to see how the firm fits into a value creation-e-management is different because doing it work requires the e-engineering of business eco-systems, e-management demands the ability to be connected to thousands of inputs about specific changes among many industry participants , such as suppliers , customers, employees, competitors, media and shareholders.

Effective e-management requires the ability to monitor developments that can change with unusually high frequency. However, it is also essential that e-managers distinguish between the few meaningful inputs and the many inputs that have limited significance, ability to sustain organizational change, effectie e-managers monitor changes in their markets. So, instead of e-commerce organizations need to employ talent e-managment staffs to help them to manage overall e-commerce organizations. E-leading staffs (HRM) is another main HRM need. E-leaders need to know how to design online brochures, e.g. online brochures simply involved putting a company's market materials on the web. in order to attract or persuade online buyers visit its websites and choose the most right price of product to buy easily. E-leaders need to lead front-office transactions which involved putting customer facing customers , such as placing on order on the web when leaving back-office activities, such as order fulfillment unchanged.

E-leaders also need to integrate online online purchase transactions in which a firm actually linked its front -office and back -office systems and processes in a fashion, e.g. most companies have developed online brochures , in order to let online advertisement tool to attract e-buyer individual purchase choice from its webstores. Hence, future any e-commerce organizations must need (HRM (e-leaders and e-managers) to help them to bring innovation in order to achieve maximize profit aim. So, internet webstores, e-leaders , e-managers may be future e-commerce organization main resources. So, e-commerce organizations, manages are actors at three levels: In the front line , as entrepreneurs, in the middle , as facilitators, and integrators, at the top as institution builders.

Hence, future new economical society, it creates e-commerce organizations number increases, when consumers began to accept online purchase transaction activities. Hence, it causes e-commerce began to feel internet (e-webstores, e-leaders, e-managers), they will be the most influential resources (intangible knowledge managment and tangible URM both resourcees to influence their success or failure.

● Why doe e-commerce organization believe (e-webstore design, e-leaders and e-managers) will be main organizational resources?

The most important question: It asks when e-buyers visit their webstores, wo are their target customers and shich needs of theirs are their trying to satisfy? For exap,e many airlines , e.g. American airlines, China airlines began to feel online e-tickets sale channel is more easily than paper ticket shop sale channel, because many air passengers began to accept e-ticket/ online ticket purchase choice more than visiting airline shops . They feel that they do not want to waste time to visit airline shops. They like to pre-book to buy e-ticket to pay from the airline e-websote conveniently. Hence, e-webstore design knowledge management , e-leaders and e-management webstore management skill will be future any one e-commerce organizations their main tangible and intangible resources (assets) to help their e-commerce businesses development.

On conclusion, I believe that the current economy is not a high-tech economy or an internet economy, not an m-commerce economy , but instead customer econoomy. Customers need to gather with information and access, they are demanding, fair, global price, they are demanding that compares deal with them using the distribution channel , they choose manufacturing direct and through dealers and retailers. Base on those factors, they encourage future many e-commerce organizations cause organization change traditional resouce concept, such as land, capital equipment, tangible resource began to change to e-commerce organization's intangibel and tangible resource, such as knowledge management to e-online web store design skills, e-leaders and e-managers e-stores sale management strategy and e-buyer product research and brochure online advertisement design skill. All of these knowledge management skill will be future organizations' main resources to help them to create new economic competition effort.

CHAPTER TWO

Organization efficient using resources economic method

Resources needers may include societies needers ,e.g. government house material householders , electricity , water , natural resources needers, schools, public houses , land number and area needs etc. as well as business organiztions , office building material, office, plant, land area, number need, equipment facilities limited number . So, when global office and plant business users need to buy more land, equipment materials etc. and electricity , water. Social resources number reduces to bring resourcee shortage challenge causes. Have they have shortage relationship (resource demand number is more than supply number) between social resources need and business resource need? I shall attempt to explain this question as below:

I assume global business organization number increases, they will need many natural resources, e.g. water, electricity, gas, land to supply for office, plant building , material and staff office electricity, gas, plant , office daily essential power need. So, when global business organizations number increases, they may need to use much raw material and natural resources for equipment facility, office plant building material, even day office, plant electricity , gas power, staff drinking water etc. basic office operational needs, when global business organizations number increase.

The question concerns whether they will cause natural resources shortage to supply to social need , when global business organizatins number increases. First, I shall explains what social resources needers mean as below:

● Social resource are defined as any concrete or symbolic term that can be used as an object of exchange among people (Foa & Foa, 1980), money, information, goods and services both tangible items , such as are ususally defined the assessment of social need is of central allocation between organization needers and social citizen needers both stakeholders. So, when global human birth rate and life time increases, population number will increase, then their social resources need are also increasing, if global organizaions and population number are increasing in the same time, due to earth natural resources has limit number to supply in order to satisfy organizations and families daily resources need, e.g. building material resources are used to build either to build offices, plants or private houses , public house, lands resources are used either to build private or public houses or offices , plants , water is supplied to either office staffs drinking or families drinking, electricity , gas resources are limited to supply either offices plants use or families private or public houses use. Hence, due to all of earth, but in the same time, global offices , plants, government organizations and families numbers both stakeholders number is continue increasing. They have possible to encounter natural resources shortage issue when natural resources are using much, but they can nt manufacturers to increase by human easily.

● Can responding to resource scarcity help some kinds business grow?

Foe example, the food and agricultural business organizations, e.g. supermarkets, restaurants, they must send plactic material to manufacture plactic bags to supply to supermarket buyers to carry fruits, breads, mil, etc. foods when consumers need to buy the kinds of foods in any supermarkets, if plactic material supply number is decreasing, then a lot plactic bags can not supply to let buyers to carry their foods, due to plactic bags number is shortage , it will cause any supermarket buyers feel inconvenient when they need plactic bags to carry their foods, they choose to buy the kind of foods from supermarket to themselves homes.

So, if plactic bags manufacture material i shortage, it can not be manufactured to plactic bags to supply to global supermarket organizations. Then, the one supermarket can provide enough plactic bags to let them to carry their foods from supermarkets to themselves homes conveniently. The focus on plactic bag resource scareity is not impossible to occur to supermarket organization case. If families are often using plactic bag to carry rubbish daily at home. Then, plactic bags number can not increase to satisfy global supermarkets food plactic bags and families themselves homes rubbish plactic bags both stakeholders need. Plastic bags can not be manufactured to supply to manufacture lot plactic bags supply to satisfy global families rubbish plactic bags home users and supermarkets food plactic bas users needs. Consequently, plactic bags prices may be influenced to increases, when plactic bags demand increases, but supply decreases. It is one good exaple to explain why plactic bag manufacturered material supply decreases, it may influence plactic bags number decreases and price increases, because families home rubbish plactic bags and supermarket food plastic bags need both increase.

Consequence, supermarket cost may be influenced , due to plastic bags number also increase much, if one day shortage of plactic manufacturing material supply number is shortage. So, it seems that food plastis bags using number, they have close relationship to impact supermarket food plastic bags price, if supermarkets lack enough plastic bag number supplies, then they need to increase food price, even the supermarket may lose customers , if it can not supply plastic bags to let them to use the supermarket itself plastic bags to carry fruits, ,ilk, soft drinks conveniently. Hence, plastic bag material may be one kind of important natureal resource for supermarkets, because any one consumer may be influenced to choose another supermarket when he/she feels the another supermarket can supply plastic bags to let him/her to carry on fruits, milks, soft drinks conveniently.

Another kind of natureal resource , such as steel material for restaurants , steel material can help global restaurants to manufacture kniefs, glass sups for restaurants customers to eat food or drink , if much steels are used to manufactured cars product to satisfy car drivers‘ driving lesiure need , then it may also influence restaurants s' knieves, glass cups price increases, due to cost increase, restaurants need to increase food price to compensate its knief, glass cups price. even, many families feel need to buy many gloass cups to drink water, then it may also influence global glass cups price increase. If one day steel material is shortage , this kind of natural resource must influence restaurants glass cups , knief cost increases. So, their general food price may be influenced to increase. It is not fair to global restaurants food consumers.

Hence, it explains resource shortage may influence some kinds of business cost increases, as well as consumer foods, products services price increases. It means that " resource shortage may influence some kinds of businesses cost increases".

In fact, in our societies, natural resource shortage may influence any kinds of business cost increases, w.g. car manufacturing industry, if one day stell manufacturing material is shortage. it will cause many car manufacturers can not buy enough steels to manufacture cars. When, global car buyers number increases, but global cars number can not increase rapidly, due to steel material can not supply enough. Then, cars prices may be influenced to raise. SO, it seems that steel resource shortage may bring reasonable chance to let global car manufacturers to raise cars prices. When , global car buyes ' new car purchase needs are increasing, hence, natural resource shortage may influence some kinds of business produce prices increase in possible, when the kind of product , such as many people begin to chose to buy new cars, more than second hand cars. The, when steel material supplies shortage, it may influence new car price increases in global can market.It means that any organizations ought not waste natural resource. Otherwise, it may influence their cost increases.

Environmental resource scarcity would likely have been adaptivve in the human evolitionary parst, resources in the environment and organization resource shortage problem might alsoo effect how satisfied they were. Hence, organizations in virtually every industry face the challenge of new managing resources effectively. The influence would run the other way instability as rival, such as big data platforms for e-commerce organizations, e.g. e-book publishers, online sellers. Big data platforms lift limitations on the size of computing resources that can be applied for data, in other words, data storage and e-commerce organizations can significantly influence computing efficiency.

Hence, organizational resources may also influence computer industry information gathering intangible resources, if the electronic books publish, or online electronic commerce product sellers can gather the most up-date consumer individual purchase behavioral data in short time daily rapidly. Then, they collect the most accurate electronic books readers or the kind of online product buyers past purchase choice in order to judge whther which topics of books are the most popular or which kinds of product to the most popular to let them to implement sale strategy, e.g. whether which topic of e-books prices need to be increased ot decreased, whether which kinds of products prices need to be increases or decreased. So, the big data gathering speed is the technology resource to e-commerce market organizations.

In behavioral economic view , any organizations can attempt to apply behavioral economy method to use resources efficiently. Organizational excellence framework performance measurement takes a systematic approach . One of the most effective ways of using resources and minimizing that use of work. Calculating task cost in the most efficient economic method to help organizations to reduce cost and avoid resources waste, e.g. using resource management software, technology, planning and taking a systematic approach , which aims to manage the most efficient steps to follow to finish or implement each task in the most shor time as well as avoiding excess employees number.

Organizational resource efficiency means using the organization's limited resources in a sustainable manner when minimising impacts on the organization performance. It allows the organization to create more with less and to deliver greater value with less money. HR, raw material, technology input to carry on any organizational resources efficiently ? Management is the process of using organizational resources to achieve organizational goals of using organizational resources to achieve organizational goals effectively and efficiently through planning , organizing , leading and controlling. An efficient organization makes the most productive use of its resource in the most short time and the most eficiency and the least cost aspects.

● What is efficient use of resources to any organizations in economics? Economic efficiency implies an economic state in which every resource is optimially allocated to serve each individual or entity in the best way when minimizing waste and inefficiency. whan an economy is economically efficient, any changes made to assist one entity would harm another . Hence, budget how much spending on resources, e.g. employee saley, office and/or plant technological equipment facilities , before making resource expenditure spending decision. Budget is essnetial to help the organization to deduce resource using and excess purchase waste since budget and resource of organizations have interlock or interconnet relationship. If the organization can make exact udget, then it can avoid excess expenditure or waste resource to use. So, organizations need to acquire a talented resource pool , that can lead projects to success, when any kinds of resources are achieved to be supplied to use inn enough . For example, using an effective enterprise resource management system that delivers capabilities. Regardless of the approach and tools used, organizations must determine how to balance to use any kinds of resources efficiently. Thus, in organizational efficient resource using behavioral economy view, the organizational efficiency factor means that influences the efficiency of the organization's use if its resources can be both internal and external, e.g. how implementing strategic plans, they may include selecting what methods and resources to use, and leadning employees on guideline, working in coalitions with organizations around to deliver those needs in the most resource efficient way.

In organizational studies, resource managemetn is the efficient and one resource management technique of resource leveling, of finding the answers to the question, how to use available resource efficiently, effectively and economically ot organization resource expense. SO , resource management is the process of allocating resources and allocating.

● What is meant by economic using of resource to organizations?

Economic resources are the factors used in producing goods or providing services. Economic resources can be divied into human resources, such as labors and management, and non humann resource, such as land, capital , goods, finished resources and technology , for example, natural resource is a key input in the production process that stimulates economic growth. Natural resources have limited direct economic use in satisfying human need, but transforming them into goods and services enhances their economic value to the socirty. So, if the country has many organizations know how to use their natural resources input in that production processes. Then, they can create themselves economic benefits directly and attribute economic benefit to society indirectly.

Thus, the types of economic organizations can be identified, there are subsistence recipreocal exchange with subsistence, peasant with primary reliance on self-produced food, but containing some exhange elements, market-commercial , redistribution or state socialist. Thus organizations need to learn hoe to use themselves organizational resources efficiently. Organizational resources are all assets that are to a firm for use during the production process. The four basic types of organizational resources are human, monetary, raw material and capital. Organizational resources are combined , used and transformed into finished products during the production process. So, a business that understands how to use resources efficiently. resource management is the process of allocating resources in order for a company to grow easily.

Organizational economic is used to study transactions within individual firms and determine management approach to managing resources. It is broken down into thee major subjects: agency theory, transaction cost economic and property rights theory. Agency theory is a priinciple that is used to explain and resolve issues in the relationship between business principles and their agents. Most commonly, that relationship is the one between shareholders as principles, and company executives as agents. Agency theory is used to understand the relationship between agents and principals. The agent represents the principal in a particular business transaction and is expected to represent the best interests of the principal without regard for seld interest. So, when the relationship between shreholders and company executives is kept the best.

Transaction cost economic is understood as alternative modes of organizing transactions (governance structure, such as markets, firms and bureaus) that mininize transactions costs. This, cost is the primary determinant of such as firm's decision whether it is the most right (the best) or the worst decision. It will influence the firm ho to spend resource behavior. The cost other than the money price that are incurred in trading good and service. SO, if the organization can often make the best decision to carry on any activites. It will avoid to waste resources efficiently. For example, if transaction cost influces the commission, paid to a stockbroker for completing a share deal and booking fee charges when purchase concert tickets. The cost of travel and time to complete an exhange , it means that transaction cost. So if the organization can make the best or the most reasonable decision to carry on any business activities. Then, its transaction cost can be influenced to reduce the most level in order to bring resources economic benefit. e.g. sunk costs are indpeendent of any event and should not resulting from economic trade in a market.

Property right theory means contracted choice, through ownership, property rights theour clarifies the firm's boundary choice. The maon egal property rights are the right of possession, the righ tof excession. So, for the efficiency of property rights al scarce resources are owned by someone. IN the right property rights approsed to the theory of the firm, I assume that in the case of sale ownership by party-property rights define the theoretical and legal ownership of resources and how resources can be used by organizatin. So, above three major organizational theories can assist organizations to know how to spend resources efficiently.

CHAPTER THREE

The relationship between resource shortage and consumer behavior

Whether formal strategy implement can avoid formal technical measurement of scale and concentrates on the loca resource mobilization using aspect os small, medium and large organization? What does resource mobilization strategy mean? Resource mobilization refers to all activities involved in sesuring new and additional resources for your organization. It also involves making better use of and maximizing , existing resources.What are the stepd in resource mobilization?

Firstly, any organizations need to plan od designing a resource moilization strategy and action plan, secondary , finding key elements of a resource mobilization strategy, thirdly,act of practical step to implementatin, fourth identify, fifth step, engagement, sixth step, negotiate, eventh step, manage and report, final step, communicating results.

What are the source of resource mobilization to any organizations? For example includes spreading flyers, holding community meetings, and recruiting volunteers. Material may include financial and physical capital, like office space, money, equipment, and supplies . Human resources, such as labour experience, skills and expertise in a certain field.

How does an entrepreneur mobilize resources? To exploit opportunities, entrepreneurs monilize and recombine a variety of resources, such as financial capital (e.g. cash, ot loan from a bank , human capital e.g. skills from a employees, and social capital e.g. information obtained from social contracts. Hence, the overall objectives of the resource mobilization strategy is to secure the necessary funds to deliver on the source mobilization strategic outcomes. To achieve this accurate resource used number and expenditure budget and emergency appeals will need sufficient preditable and contrributions. So, the aim of resource mobilization strategy outlines how secretariat will organize the process of prioritising, plannin, selecting projects, monitoring: broadening the resource channels, as well as coordinating with staffs for mobilising and effectively utilizing resources.

So, the genesis of resource mobilization strategy is a good, solid strategic plan, it should articulate activities that are more routine in nature and can be finded through the organizational internal efficient resource mobilization. Resource mobilization refers to all activities involves in securing . These new directions or new business opportunities are pursued using a distinct resource mobilization strategy .

On conclusion , an efficient resource mobilization plan is a term resource mobilization, it refers to all activities undertaken by an organizations to secure new and additional financial, human and material resources to advance its mission. Inherent in efforts to mobilize resources is the drive for organizational sustainability . So, resource mobilization is about an organization getting the resources that are needed to be able to do the work it has planned. Resource mobilization is more that just fundraising, it is about getting a range or resources from a wide range of resource providers for donors, through a number of different mechanisms. How does an entrepreneur mobile resources? To exploit opportunities, entreprensurs mobilize and combine a variety of resources, such as financial captial , e.g. cash or loans from a bank, human capital e.g. skill from an employee and social capital e.g. information obtained from social contract.

Why do organizations need resource mobilization strategy? The reasons may include: The principles of resource mobilization wih examples, it focuses on forging partnerships built on trust and mutual accountability . So, as to attract adequate and more predictable contributions, with the future goal of sustainability, it refers to all undertaken by an organizatin to secure new and additional financial , human and material resource to advance its mission, in efforts to mobilize resources is the drive for organizational sustainability, community mobilization is the process of bring together as many stakeholders as possible to raise people's awareness of and demand for a particular programme to assist in the delivery of resources and services, and to strengthen community participation for sustainability an dself -reliance, resource mobilization is often referrred t as " new business creaating chance" , the organization has a strong, yet flexible structure , such as writing proposal how to spend the least respurce expenditure in order to achieve the most satisfactory effective result to the organization.

Hence, developing a resource mobilization strategy plan , as the source of new business opportunities to the social and behavioral change considerations must be needed the organization as well as resource mobilization target at a minimum level should be needed to raise at transformational change happen on the ground and advocate for the products and may have to develop new business proposal.

● Can resource mobilization change improve organizational performance?

I believe that resource mobilization can help any organizations to change or improve performance to the better, even the best. I shall explain as below:

What are the sources of organizational change? Change originates in either the external or internal environments of the organization. External sources include political, social, technological or economic environment, externally motivated change may involve government action, technology development, competition , social values and economic variables.

How do organizational resources affect change? Results indicate that organizations possessing greater stocks of historically valuable resources were much less likely to engage in adaptive strategic change, but also that this resoure-driven towards change tended to have a even beneficial effect on performance . Wonder of organizational change management is easier spoken about than achieved by resource mobilization strategic in possible? Can create enterprise level value by effective process for resource allocation?

The key to success involves managing organizational change , so it leads to real and lasting improvements, tailoring to resource allocation how mobilization strategy. So, nowadays, organizational capacty for change: Increasing change capacity and avoiding change overload, organization, today risk is overcommitting resources, resulting in an overload condition wih which it how allocates its resources to tbe used efficiently or inefficiently. For example, on new government regulations, ne products development or growth aspect, organizational change efforts often run into some form of human resistance. First, management staffed its human resource departments with spend most of that time in efficiency. So, whether how organizational change is better, it depends on how it changes its old resources, e.g. human resource, facility, equipment resources, even management time resources to change new improvement resources change to be better . It means providing the resources, budget, authority, credibility and commitment for the effort to truly organizational change on improvement.

● Why does organizational resource budget need?

For example, managing a human resource department involves budget planning and execution . The human resources budger refers to the finds that how HR allocates to all HR processes. Unit should include in an HR budget. It may include: number of employees, projected for next year, benefits cost increases or decreases, salary cost increases or decreases, projected turnover rate, calculation, actual cost incured in the current year, new employee welfare benefits. programs planned, other changes in policy, business strategy , it may impact costs on HR cost aspect. So, an organization needs to budget whether it will have how much on what kinds of resources spending aspect, including human resources, facility, equipment and water , electricity etc. natural resource , it budget is a tool used for planning and controlling financial resources. It is a guideline for future plan of action, espressed in financial terms within a set of period time, knowing organization's priorities, objectives and goals helps it prepare organization resource budget.

Effectively leveraging people and budget, resource management is critical for organizations to ensure . They are optimizing and allocating resources to the right initiations, e.g. from a human resource perspective, the data needed to create a new budget include the following number of employees, working arrangement tasks time, management time, employee salary cost, due to costs that only impact the human resource department and impacts the entire organization both aspects. So, efficient HR cost budget can help refine goals that reflect realistic resources and how memebers of the organization to use fund because employee retirement can be expensive and it can b increased or decreased expense in any time, when the month needs increase or decrease employees number to any departments. It depends on whether tasks rate is needed to increase or decrease. So, an organization's HR cost budget can help how it makes the most accurate HR resource expenditure.

Organizational facility, equipment, shop, office, warehouse space resource budget why is important. Office space is as an enabling resource, equipment and furniture to enhance the organization's ability to achieve efficient operations and activities of the best organizational performance. In view of this analysis, facility planning personal would be one important factor to influence whether the organizatin can spend the least expenditure to use its resource. During business growth, any facility equipment, office , shop, warehouse space must increase , moreover staff puts increasing number on existing resources, so be sure to budget in order to make another option is to least equipment instead of buying it, whether you need moving insurance for important equipment and machinery, set budget to help prevent overspending.

All of the tasks that are include in maintaining a facility, such as equipment maintenance and building facilities whether are needed to improve, facility oversight, warehouse and special equipment whether is qpproriate space for customer service and uses resource dynamic of an organization's work patterns with work. It depends partly on the resources an organization is willing to invest or not, when it feels this facility resources are very important to influence its performance.

● What does organization office , shop , warehouse space resource management strategy?

Organization and using space must be land resource, if the organization can manage how to use its space in efficiency, then it can improve service performance or productive efficiency. Space management can be defined as a practice where an organization manages its physical space invnetory which includes tracking , control, supervision and utilization, planning of the space available. So, space management is the mangement of an organization's physical space inventory. Ths involves the tracking of how much space an organization has managing occupancy information and creating spatial plans. So, one efficient space resource using organization, it needs to undertake annual property assessment reviews, leverage individual projects to drive portfolio evoluation applya planning methodology on all project rises, utilize planning to define direction and scope focus on mathematics before graphics, define and collect only the required data on warehouse, shops, office, buildind space using aspect. For example, a space management ffice can give the organizatin an accurate picture of how many employees , it needs to have space for an average day, and show it the trends of demand for this space across weeks and months. This can help the organization to determine how many permanent desks could be converted to hot desks in office, warehouse or shop , saving space. For example, space managementin retail aspect, it is the process of managing the floor space adequately to facilitate the customers and to increase the sale.

Shop space management is very crucial in retail as the sales volume and gross profitability depends on the amount of space used to generate those sales. Space management is a multi-step process that requires data gathering, analysis , forecast and strategizing. In prective, it involes creating a space management system that occupants throughout your organization, so whether the organization realizes it or not, every organization needs to know how to manage its space one way or another , if it hopes to improve its service or productive performance. Make use of these strategic space management and planning techniques, efficient and an unplanned, unmanaged office is not likely to magically transofrm into a well organized of productivity. So, space management is the management of an organization's physical space inventoty , employee working environment, shop product putting sheleves locatin, equipment, desk putting location. All of this tangible space physical factor may influence overall organizational service and/or productive performance and /or sale performance. So, space may be an organization's land usng resource because any organization's land using space must be limited size, they must have land space using shortage challenge if their products stock number increases, but warehouse space can not increase or shop products shelves number can not increase, but product sale number increases.

● The relationship netween organization behavior and resource using management accounting

Has organizational behavior and resource spending, they have close cause and effect direct relationship ? When one organization can perform better, whether it represents that it must spend much resource to use or when it perform poor, it represents that it must not spend much resource to use. Organizational behavior is a field of study that investigates the impact that organizational psychology and human resource management, the cause and effect relationship.

How organizational behavior effects an oganization? Organizational behaviors propose that inventives are motivational factors that are crucial for employees to perform well. It changes the way people make decisions, e.g. decision to increase or decrease resources to use, when the organization feels that it has resource shortage or excess. However, businesse that are able to encourage risks in decision making within the company culture can enhance innovation and creativity.

In fact, organizational behavior has four main elements, people, structure, technology and external environment. So , tangible and intangible resources may influence organization behavior when it is needed to change by management, e.g. human behavior in a work environmen and determines its impacts on job structure, performance, communication, motivation, leadership etc. for example, when the manager has less time to prepare how to organize this meeting process to his client. His short managing meeting plan time , intangible time resource, it can influence his business proposal to be either accepted or rejected to this client. So , time resource whether it is enough or not. It can influence this manager's client proposal meeting whether it is accepted or rejected in possible.

Every employee behavior can determine the importance of group departments in business productivity. So, it seems that resources whether they are enough , they can impact on employee's performance. As a result, managers are able to maintain better relation with their employees by effective utilization of human resource. So, cause and effect relationship plays an important rolw in how an individual is likely to behave in a enough tangible and intangible resource provided or not enough organization.

CHAPTER FOUR

Ecommerce organization resource management strategy

Why does in this e-commerce organization situation, online webstore speed must be the most important factor to influence its sale success. Information technology internet speed, online webstore design, online transation convenience transaction feeling (tangibale and intangible both resource factors) may influence its future clients number ?

In behavioral economic view, any organizations must need to use resources to carry on any business or working activities. Resources may include: management time to managements, working time to employees, information technology etc. office computer to administration, factory equipment to plant workers, plant or warehouse land space to logistic delivery or goods shelves, electricity, gas , water to workplace , even, employees number. HR to any department tasks. So, it seems that before any organization can finish any activities, they must need enough resources supply in order to satisfy any activities need. If the organization overall itself , even overall society. I shall explain as below:

For ecommerce organizatin example, any online trading firms must need to own high speed internet information technology resource to supply to any one technologic staff store to pay visa to buy any product in the most short time rapidly. So, its online store website speeds must need to be very fast in order to avoid to delay any country clients to carry on online transaction. If the ecommerce business organization can not support efficient, high speed internet service to let any countries online buyers to satisfy its online webstore purchase service. Then, any countries' online buyers may choose another online store to replace to buy its similar product easily.

Hence, convenient webstore online purchase service much be very important to influence this online webstore organization. It seems that technologic online internet resource must be the most influential factor to influence this online websore organization clients number. If its online website store can not supply rapid online purchase speed to let any one country to buy its products from its webstores rapidly. Then, its clients number may be influenced to reduce. So, in this e-commerce organization situation, online webstore speed must be the most important factor to influence its sale success. Information technology internet speed, online webstore design, online transation convenience transaction feeling (tangibale and intangible both resource factors) may influence its future clients number . So, judging whether the kind of resource is the most important to influence the organization's success, it depends on whether it needs to use what kind of resource to carry on its daily activities.

In fact, one organizational change has relationship to whether its reponses can have enough supply as well as its behavior can be influenced by the resources variable , the scarcity of any kinds of resources are supplied to be used. So, I believe that whether any kinds of resources are scarcity in the organizational environment, how much they are used, these any kind of resources can bring relationship to influence how organizational perceptions, interpretations and responses.

How an ecommerce organization resource affects society?

Why has online webstore's information technology resource close relationship t influence online buyers number and social job chance?

Organizational impact to the effect on an organization has any reponses to influence how on society chance. However, organizations can also have a positive impact on the economic satisfaction of a town. More oe less jobs supply to the wociety, which can be influenced by whether the organization can have effort to buy how much resources to be used in order to carry on itself any business activities. Hence, it seems that if the organization, such as the above online website sale product organization, if it can have enough money to employ web design professional to help it to design attractive website stores to let attract online buyer purchase choice, as well as paid higher internet service fee to improve its fee to improve its online internet speed in order to let any countries online customers can still click its website rapidly, even in busy online click time. Many people click computer mouse to enter ecommerce website stores in the same time.

Then, any one won't choose another websites stores to replace its online sale service easily. Even, if it can buy many advanced computers to let its staffs can use the best quality computers to follow any client's ourchase transaction in short time. When , they confirm that whether the client's visa card payment can accept and what product he has paid to buy from its webstore. Then, the staff can know where the accurate address of the country , the client's product can be delivered rapidly. It will avoid to delay any product delivery. So, if this online store seller can have enough internet information technology source to support its whole computer information department staffs to wrk efficiently. Then, it can increase more online transaction chance in success. Consequently, it can grow up its online sale business, it will create many new potisition, due to its computer information technology department must need to increase employees to help it to deal any countries online buyers online purchase service transactions and online product sale delivery service immediately in order to avoid online product delivery service to global online buyers. So, it can bring more job chance if this online webstore organization can have enough effort to buy high technological computer information products to let its online customer service staffs to use in order to improve online product delivery service store to let global many online buyers' attention . Consequently, it can apply online webstore purchase channel to apply website purchase channel to persuade many global online buyers online purchase choice to its webstore easily. So, it seems that this online webstore's information technology resource has close relationship t influence online buyers number and social job chance.

How do organizational resources affect organizational change?

IN general, resoults indicate that organizations possessing greater stocks of historically valuable resources were much less likely to engage in adaptive strategic change, but also that this resource-driven disinclination towards change tended to have a begin or even beneficial effect on performance . So, in general, if one organization lacks any one of these three important resources. It can influence this organization's performance to worse, they many include: human resource , financial resource, phycial resources and information resource. However, managers are responsible to acquiring and managing the resources to accomplish goals. If the organization can have enough resources to be used. It can bring positive impact to influence its overall organizational performance, even, when it has not any resource scarcity, it can avoid negative impacts on the society, such as increasing jobs chance. Hence, scarcity of capital, human and social resources to be provided to the organization, it will influence the organizational structure changes, even employee individual work attitude is influenced to change worse, when he/she can not have the best resources to be used in order to raise efficiency or improve performance more easily.

How to build organizatonal resource using right psychology

The psychology of management is the branch of psychology studying mental features of the person and its behavior in the course of planning, organization management and the control of joint activity. The human factor is considered as the central point in the psychology of management as its essence and a core. Hence , organizational psychology plays a very important rolw at the time or recruitment very important role at the time of recruitment taking disciplinary action or resolving disputes between employees. HR focus and expertise mainly lies in dealing with people . So , it makes sense that the study of the human mind, how to use organizational resources efficiently.

The organizational side of pschology is more focused on understanding how organizations affect individual behavior, organizational structures , social norms, management styles and role expectations are factors that can influence how people behave within organizations. In general, industrial organizational psychologists use psychological principles and research methods to solve problems in the workplace and improve the quality of life (e.g. avoiding often waste industrial resources in manufacturing process aims). They study workplace workplace productivity and management and employee working styles. They get a feel for the morale and personality of a company or organization, e.g. suggesting to use skills and knowledge relating to psychology how to reduce same productivity level, but the organizational resources can be reduced to use. It is one kind the most efficiency resources using method to any kind of organizations.

On conclusion, industrial and organizational psychologists will often use science to study human behavior organizations and the workplaces. Their aims to help organizations to reduce excess resource using in any manufacturing process in order to reduce cost. Employers who need to attempt to learn how employees use resources to do work activities, it can bring these advanaages : learning how to use neuroscience to attract the right talent, retain high performing employees, because any organizations' resources will be used in order to manufacture any products or work activites by any employees in any time.

Employees are the ones who get the job done. They know how the organization and especially ho w their specigif team works best. So any one employee may be the important factor to influence the amount of resource use, any organizational resource use amount, it has close relationship to any employee work behavior. Moreover, resources, that is , group-level resources associated with shared relationship that foster a quality exchange of information and interaction between individuals within the workplace , helping any one employee to learn more about on the job training, use employee training optios to ensure department leader optimizes the employees' motiviation and potential retention. Aim to give opinions to employees to know how to avoid resource using waste method to achieve cost saving aim to the organization.

CHAPTER FIVE

Robots whether can help organizations to avoid resource waste

To judge whether robots can help any organizations to avoid resources waste behavior. We need to know whether robots can own recyle function. How do robots helpthe environment? Robots can help reduce waste that is implemented by effectively sorting materials that can be recycled and put to use again. They can even help sort waste materials quickly and move efficiently than humans reduce the input power amd cost unsociated with such processes. However, robots also may help business organizations with recycling, instead of natural environment . For example, tobots may help organization facility cut operate resource cost and allowed to take on a second load of recyclables to sort throgh.

How robotic technology help organizations reduce waste?

Advanced software has made it easier to plan out routes that can efficiently guide waste collecting the waste and recycling materials that need to be collected. It also makes collection more fuel efficient and reduces energy usage to any offices, plants, warehouses, business organizations. It seems that robots can help organizations to bring recycling advantages. We should definitely keep on teaching robots to recycle our waste, e.g. clean robotics makes waste management smart with a robotic trash can that automatically separates used and not used materials in workplace environment.

How to use technology to help reduce waste?

There is no financial incentive to reduce waste. One of a few manufacturers of AI (arificial intelligence) powered recycling robots. We can imagine a future where waste-collectig robots will move through air land, and water, cleaning our natural environment, workplace environment conveniently. For example, now robots are being put on duty to help solve the environment pollution, material waste, recycling challenges. AI assisted robotis technology that can work with humans in workplace organizational environment to have robots to do a better job at sorting garbage and reduce the building materials is wasted, sorting trash is a dirty and dangerous job, recycling robots may help human to do thin kind of sorting trash job, even further atomic bombs soon could be delivered over intercontinental distances aboard " pick a back" multi-stage rockets by robotis assistance. So, in our future, robotic can be applied on those avoiding resource waste job aspects, such as degradation and resource depletion , reduce , reuse, recycle and recover, have always been needed to avoid resource waste to future global business organizations. When, AI machine learning and robotics could help us , more efficiently organization, digital tools and new business models.

How green robots are helping with environmental sustainablity?

Robots can help reduce waste that is implemented by effciently sorting materials that can be recycled and put to use again. They can even help sort waste materials quickly and most efficiently than humans reducing the input power and cost associated with such processes.

How robots may help organizations to avoid resource waste?

Waste robotics autonomous recycling technology integrates advanced waste technology to avoid the costly deployment to any organizational users, e.g. the clean sea robot is an autonomous, electric floating aqua-droue that sweeps and collects plastic trash that has collected in coastal areas. It uses a has collected in coastal areas . It uses a combination of computer vision and remote sensing basd on 3D laser scanning technologies . So, clean sea robots can bring sea environmental protection advantages to global seas. Future global sea environment protection organization must need its clean sea tasks helping.

Instead of clean sea rubbish aspect, robots can also help organizations to do digital waste management tasks, digital technologies and their current use in waste management transparent, more economic and more resource-efficient processes, better souring of current important robotis digital waste manaement, technological trends, are robotics,the internet of things, cloud, digital rubbish robotic can help organizations to reduce digital rubbsh easily. then, any organizational digital system can do more efficient tasks daily. Hence, robotics can help e-commerce organizations to do digital resource waste management tasks in order to provide high efficient online purchase services to any countries online buyers in short time.

How robots are applied to reduce waste in hotel organizations?

Reducing waste in hotels in within reach with the help of digital technologies. How are robots used in hotels? Throughout the hotels, robots are deployed to provide information, front desk services, storeage services as well as check in and cleck out services , with technology including voice and facial recognition. An example, of artifical intelligence in the hospitality industry is the use of AI to deliver in-person customer service. The robot is able to provide tourist information to customers who interact with it. Most impressively, it is able to learn from human speech and adapt to individuals. waste management in hotels is important or it is getting increasingly difficult to dispose of waste. Therefore, hotel resource management robots can help hotels to decrease cost of waste disposal as the start with: Using refillable dispensers for soaps, shampoos and conditioners. Could hotel service robots help the hospitality industry on resource management of robotized hotels, e.g. avoding food waste in hotel robotized hotels, example restaurants robotics technology can help chefs measure, manage and reduce food wase. Morevoer, a restuaurant robots do not get waste and can perform to help chels measure, manage and reduce food waste easily. From a human resource management point of view, in that sense, robotisation may help automation and hotels to improve it service and reduce restaurant food waste cost.

Can Robotic Help Warehouses To Avoid Resource Waste On Behavioral Economic View

● Behavioral economy view whether robotic can help
warehouse to avoid time and human resource
waste

IN fact,robts are being used in different types manufacturing to create more efficiency with fewer resource. Robots also reduce errors, to leass waste is produced. Less waste is produced and the robots are able to final and separate the small parts more efficiently than human hands can. For example, on environment recycled aspect, robots can help reduce waste that is incinerated by efficiently sorting materials that can be recycled quickly and more efficiently than humans reducing the input poser and cost control with such processes. So, robots can bring positive affect the environment, because robots use less energy and produce less waste.

As a whole, there are multiple benefits to using robots to fight climate change,e.g. robots can prevent pollution and emissions through careful monitoring optimize the manaufacturing processes to reduce energy consumption. Moreover, robots can help with recycling, the use of robots allows facility operators some new flexibility. Most technologies used in recycling allow to sort materials. The sensing robots (sensoes) allow robots to receive information about a certain measurement of the environment , or internal components. This is essential to robots to perform their tasks, and act upon any changes in the environment to calculate the appropriate response.

● How Amazon warehouse applies logistic robots to help
it to waste resource waste

Hence, although robots can take our jobs, because they can help organizations to avoid resource waste, and it can bring negative effect to influence we lose jobs. ON behavorioral economic view, robots can help employers to reduce employees number, but it won't influence organizational overall performance to be worse or inefficiency, such as Amazon warehouse applies logistic robots to assist workers to deliver the right kind of goods to put on every correct shelf number position rapidly every day. Hence, one logistic robot can replace at least 10 store workers to do goods delivery tasks every day, e.g. one store worker needs to spend one minute to find the right kind of good to deliver to prepare to arrange to deliver it to fly to overseas client. Logistic robots only need 10 seconds to find the right kind of goods from the near 200 number shelves in Amazon warehouse as well as they are putting 300 different kinds of goods on these 200 shelves in Amazon warehouse every day.

Because each logistic robot has very good memory. Each logistic robot must remember any kinds of goods , their putting number position on which shelf, e.g. when the worker needs to find the model laptop product from 300 different kinds of products,in Amazon warehouse. They are putting on 200 number shelves number following positions. IN general, human worker will need to spend about one minute to find the model of laptop product from these 200 number shelves in warehouse. For example, when one worker needs to find the brand Apple of one laptop product model: PHZ0123, when the warehouse has total 300 diferent kinds of products are putting on total 200 numbers of different shelves positions. Any one Amazon store worker must need to type this Apple brand laptop" Apple" name and its model number" PHZ0123 on the store computer as well as to search its putting on shelf number position from computer. Then, the Amazon store computer will find this laptop product to find its present putting on the correct shelf number position , e.g. 50 number of the shelf positon, or none stock record of all this model PHZ20123 laptop is sold out. So, Amazon store computer must need time to help this store worker to search this laptop product's putting on shelf number position as well as the worker needs time to walk to the right shelf number position to find this laptop product.

However, logistic robotic does not need to spend time to type this laptop product brand name and model number in order to search where it is putted on the shelf number position. The Amazon store worker only needs to speak this laptop product brand name, e.g. Apple and the kind of product, e.g.laptop and model number, e.g. PHZ0123 and its piece number, e.g. one piece number. Then, the Amazon logistic robot can follow the store worker's sound to find its past this kind of product's shelf number position memory to move to this shelf correct number position and finds it to deliver to the worker immediately. So, if the worker speaks 10 kinds f different products one time, then the logistic robotic can help this worker to find these 10 of different kinds products from their correct shelves numbers rapidly.

Hence, it seems that logistic robots can help Amazon store workers to reduce each product search time as well as logistic robots can help workers to do goods delviery tasks. So, in logistic robotic behevioral economic vire, logistic robotics can replace many workers to do product position research and delivery tasks, store workers only need to speak the kind of product name, model, brand name and delivery piece number to let the logistic robotic to know. Then, the logistic robotic can follow the store worke's sending message to find the product's past memmory in order to tell the store worker, whether the product has how many stocks on shelf, or none of stock on shelf and where is putted on . Hence, any one store worker does not need to spend much time to search where any kinds of products shelves number position are. They only need logistic robotics to help them to do any kinds of products deliver to , or 20 or more different kinds between products location and the store worker's location. It means that the store worker only needs to stay on the same location to wait the logistic robotic brings his products comes back after he speaks to let the logistic rotic to know whether which kinds of products and piece number he needs . Then, he checks the logistic robotic's all products where they are correct or not. He may put all of these different kinds of gatherng products to the lorry to prepare to send to airport to fly to another country to deliver to the overseas client's home immediately when he confirms that all goods are his correct. Hence, such as Amazon warehouse case, logistic robotics can help it to reduce many products searching time tasks and avoiding delivering wrong product to any overseas client's home rick occurence. Also, logistic robotics can reduce store workers number, because logistic robotics can replace 10 to 20 human store workers number absolutely. Otherwise, human store workers may have errors in their product search process, e.g. finding the wrong product from shelf or putting the product to the wrong shelf number position, but logistic robotics can reduce to 0 error to put wrong product on the shelf number position or spends long time to search the kind of product from the shelf number position. So, in logistic robotic behavioral economic view, robotics can help businesses to avoid products putting on wrong shelves number position error risk, reduce store workers number, reduce product shelf number position search economic time.

Chapter 11 How organization resource influences
earth resource shortage
The relationship between organization resource and earth resource in behavioral economic view, global organizations use any kinds of resource, such as office, warehouse facility building resource to build any new offices, warehouses, supermarkets, shopping centers, car parks, whether they can bring global building resources reducing number to satisfy human houses living needs, if one day building resources are facing any kinds building material is reducing number, but global applying steel, wood, brick etc. different kinds of building material number increases, when global population number is still increasingm any high houses' building materials need increase, even low wood houses' wood natural resource needs increase in order to let many people can live in the expensive wood houses. SO, it brings this question: Would wood, natural resource, steel, brick resource have shortage supply challenge, due to office, warehouse, shopping center,manufacturer, ther fixed assets number building need increases, but the same time, global houses need number also increases, when polulation increases? Can businessmen their fixed assets : offices , warehouse, shopping centers, factories, supermarkets, etc. building need bring negative impact to influence future human living house resource nu mber decreases?

I assume that global businessmen their offices, warehouses, shopping centers, hospitals, private school education organizations, supermarkets etc. business organizations their buildings number is sudden increasing high, due to many organizations can earn more profit to expand their businesses. So, they will need to spend much woods, steels, bricks etc. different kinds nature resources to build any high , height offices buildings in different countries. So, wood, steel brick etc. different kinds of offices building material need must also sudden be influenced to sudden increase by global business organizations increasing number. When global businesses organizations number increases, it will cause global high height offices number increases, because every business organizations must need to rent any building office to operate their businesses. If global has many new businesses are continue growing, they will influence offices building need in possibe, even for food business , e.g. supermarke, restaurant building material need will also increase, if the reestaurant can earn more profit, then it will need to expand itself restaurant vacancy floor to let many food customers do not need to spend long queue time to wait table in order to avoid to loss these food customers, even it will buy any shopping center location to build one or more than one restaurant to satisfy food customers need . So building material needs to the new restaurant design, it may decide to decorate all restaurant location, to feel food customers to feel more comfortable when they are sitting in its restaurant.SO, when the restaurant changes its inside design , it needs to find designers to buy any new building materials to design its restaurant to be new one in order to attract food customer choice.

● Green building reduces resource waste

I assume that global many old restaurants need to recorate their inside, or many global restaurants number increases, then any restaurants material natural resource need number may also be influenced to increase. Then, our earth building material resource for restaurants need will influence general office buildings material resource, shopping center building material resource decreases to supply. When, global many restaurants are needed to build, more building material resource is needed to be used build new restaurants or is needed to decorate to change old restaurants design . So, our earth will have much building material resources to be used to build new restaurants or they are be used to decorate the old restaurants design in order to change new restaurants design function. So, our earth building material natural resources for new or old restuarants , which must increase, when global has many restaurants need any kinds of building materials to be used to help them to build new or old restaurants. Then, they must influence natural resources of building material supply number to be reduced to satisfy any office building matierals user need, even any house building material user need, if global offices and houses number sudden increase. Consequently, due to global building material natural resource can not be produced rapidly in order to satisfy any office building, shopping center, house, supermarket etc. different kinds business organizations or private houses needs. Then, the natural resource of building resources shortage, it may influence any kinds of building material production price increases. It may influence global business organizations need to pay high price to rent office or build office, or build supermarket, or build shopping center, even any private houses prices increase, when global building material natural resource has no enough number to be supplied to satisfy builders' need in order to help any office, supermarket, shopping center, supermarket warehouse etc. business organization users to build their properties to operate their businesses. SO, these businessmen must need to spend much money for building expenditure, when they begin to do their businesses. Even, public or private house buyers also need to pay more expenditure to buy houses to live , when any kinds of building material price increases.

So, it explains why global business organizations number increases may influence global public or private houses prices increase, when our earth has no enough natural resource to be building matieral supplied to satisfy global construction properties development need. Finally, when global construction properties developers feel our earth building material natural resource encounters supply shortage challengem due to they need to pay higher price to buy any kinds of building material to help any business organizations to build their offices, restaurants, supermarkets, shopping centers, wareshouses etc. different fixed assets buildings or they need to ehlp any public or private houses buyers to build their houses. Consequently, any one businessmen or house livers must need to pay high price to buy any houses or offices , restaurants, hospitals etc. different buildings either to live or to use for business operations. Hence, it seems that they have chose resource supply surplus or shortage relationship between business organizations and private house buyers.

ON conclusion, I recommend that any business office buildings ought choose green buildings orrice, their advantages may include to avoid nature resource waste, improved indoor environment, quality of life , saving water, reduce , reuse, enhanced health, eco-friendly for life, reducing operational cost and maintenance , energy -efficient, non-renewable, vs renesable resource, keep it clean, protecting our ecosystem . Hence, green buildings can not only reduce or eliminate negative impacts on the environment, by using less water, energy, or natural resources.

Moreover, green buildings, or substainable design, is the practice of increasing the efficiency with wich buildings and their sites use energy , water and materials, and reducing impaction human health and the environments for lifecycle of a building. So, on environmental benefits of grren building aspect, it can enhance and protect bio-diversity and ecosystems , imprive air and water quality, reducing waste streams, conserve and restore natural resources, on economic benefits of green building aspect, it can reduce operating costs, improve occupant productiviity, enhance asset value and profits optimize life-cycle economic performance, on social bebefits of green building aspct, it can enhance occupant health and comfort, improve indoor air quality, minimize strain on local utility infrastracture, improve overall qualty of life.

Consequently, if any organizations can apply green building concept to design and build their offices, waterhouses, restaurants, shopping centers etc. different kinds of business green buildings, even ourselves houses design is chosen by green building concept. On behavioral economic view, green building concept is the best moethod to help us to reduce natural resource waste nowadays. Then, I beleive that our earth nature resources won't be easte easily.

CHAPTER SIX

Technology brings influences organizational changes

Can technology influence human shopping behavioral change?

Nowadays, technological development has reached mature stage, whether technological mature stage may bring positive or negative shopping emotion influence to global consumers. I shall aplly internet inventin or ecommerce shopping channel tool to explain whether internet technology can bring postive or negative influence to global consumer behavior in behavioral economic view.

Internet is a good technological tool, it brings e-commerce business chance. In fact, commonly, global has have many businessmen choose to use internet channel to carry on their products transactions between global online-buyers and their electronic websites. So, global many shoppers had begun to feel online shopping is more convenient to compare visiting shops shopping. Their shopping behaviors have been changed from internet technological tool. Global has many shoppers choose to buy any products from any overseas or local businessmen their web stores. They only need to spend time to find any businessmen their webstores to choose the most suitable products to pay visa to buy from their webstores. at homes. So, in general, global had have may shoppers had changed their shopping behaviors from visiting shops to visiting webstores at homes often.

So, it seems that internet technological tool had influenced global many shops disappear, but internet webstores will be replaced their actual shops on streets. Some of businessmen either they choose webstores to replace shops or choose websotes and shops both or still keep shops only. Hence, internet tool influences global businessmen have three kinds of products sale channels to let globa local and overseas consumers to choose how to buy their products.

However, in fact, many of global shoppers, youngers and olders had begun to accept to buy any products from webstores. They feel to spend time to leave homes to visit shops , their shopping behaviors will be wasted time to not essential part to their daily lives. Hence, since internet technological invention, it had changed many consumers their traditional visiting shops shopping habit to change to buying products from webstores channel.

However, on the one hand, internet creates webstores ecommerce shopping channel to let global many consumers do not need to leave homes to go to shopping. It brings negative visiting shops shopping emotion to global general consumers nowadays. But on the other hand, it also brings positive visiting internet webstores shopping emotion to global general consumer nowadays. So, it seems that global many consumers feel that they often do not need to spend much time to go out shopping. Many global consumers feel convenient and enjoy to choose any products to buy from different internet webstores, when the online buyer chooses the most suitable product, he she only needs to pay visa card to buy the product from the online seller's webstore conveniently at home.

Hence, online shopping can bring economic benefit to online buyers, e.g. avoiding walking time or spending transport fare to visit the shop to go to shopping, shortening or reducing shopping time to do another important matter.

On conclusion, global many consumers began feel online shopping can bring more economic benefits on shortening shopping time, avoiding transport fare spending aspect. So, online shopping will be popular shopping behavior for future long time. It may encourage global many shoppers can make rapid shopping decision in short time in order to carry on any products buying transaction to global any one online shopper in short time easily in behavioral economic view. So, global many businessmen had begun to build themselves one attraction webstore in order to persuade different countries consumers to choose to click themselves webstores from internet channel to buy any kinds of products in short time easily.

So, internet technology had changed consumers traditional shopping behaviors to build positive online shopping emotion as well as raise online sellers' any products sale chance easily in behavioral economic view.

Why and how human behavior may influence the country's economic growth or recession?

When one country has many people choose to do the same matter for one period, whether their behavior may influence the country's pvera;

economic growth or recession . I shall attempt to indicate cases toexplain their relationship as below:

For flowing rubblish behavioral case example, do you feel that when the country has many people often flow rubblish on the streets, instead of their flowing rubblish behavior may bring streets dirty? But, their flowing rubblish behavior may explain that this country has people may have enough money to buy food to ear, or enough cloths to wear, enough bottles of water to drink, even they may have enough money to buy new television, radio, refrigeraters , washing machines, desktops or laptops electronic home products from old to new to use in order to satisfy their living needs. So, when they flow old electronic home products, their flowing old home electronic products behaviors may seem that they have enough money to buy other new home electronic products to replace old home electronic products to use at homes.

However, it seems thaat this country ought have many people have jobs to do. So, many of them, they can easy to make purchase decison to flow any old home electronic products and buy any new home electronic products to use . Because this country has many people have jobs to do. So, they can often not use old home electonic products to become rubblishs to flow on streets after they had bought any kinds of new home electronic homes.

In fact, it also implies that this country's economy grows rapidly. So, many businesses can glow up rapdly. When they expanded their businesses, they must need to increase employees number in order to let they help themselves to raise productivity or serve their clients absolutely. So, when the country has many businesses can grow up, it seems that its economy must be better or it is improved to compare past. Due to many different kinds of home electronic products had been often bought to use by this country people in this period. So, this country's any streets can be observed that expensive electronic home products were flowed on streets anywhere. then, this country will have many electronic home products sellers can sell their home electronic products very easily. When this country has many people can find any kinds of jobs to do easily. So, due to unemploymen rate had been decreasing.

In behavioral economic view, as this many electronic home products rubblish country case, we can observe this country may have many people have jobs to do. So, consumption number has been increased long time. So, cheap food, or expensive home electronic products may be rubblish on any streets. This country's people , their flowing rubblish behaviors may be explained that many of people have enough jobs to do, so they have ability to buy any good taste food to eat or buy any kinds of expensive electronic home products to use. So, this country's economy may be improved for this long period. So, in behavioral economic view, when this country can have many electronic home products rubblishs are flowed on anywherer in streets frequently. It seems that this country will have many people have jobs to do, so it causes they often change old home electronic products or replaced them easily, when they have enough income to spend to buy any kinds of new home electronic products to use at homes easily. Moreover, their flowing old electronic home products behaviors also indicate that this country has many people their salaries may be increased in possible from their emplyers. When this country can have many different kinds of home electornic products are sold. It means that this country's electronic home products needs or demand had been increasing, due to many people have jobs to do and income increases to excite their living of needs also improve. Consequently, this country may seem have better economic improvement. We can observe from this country's electronic home products rubblish increasing income in theis period.

On conclusion, this country ought experience economic growth at this period. So, " flowing expensive electronic home rubblish increasing number " may seem that this country's economic growth is rapidly in this period, due to many people have jobs to do as well as salaries increase in this period.

Technology how impacts human behavior changing?

Technology how influences human behavior to bring changing? For example, online share purchase and sale transaction from smart phone brings share investor can do share buying or selling transation in any where and any time conveniently, non manual driving auto vehicle, bring car owner feels comfortable and spends free time to do other matter, e.g. reading, listening mucis in himself or herself car freely. electrical energy vehicle can help car owner to reduce air polluton and it can brings the drivers do not feel drive long time in any journeys in order to avoid air pollution for environmental protection responsible car drivers in our societies. Thus, they will drive long time in any journeys when they can drive electronic energy cars to replace oil energy cars.

However, online technology can also bring consumers can choose to stay at homes to buy any things from seller individual online webstore conveniently. Such as online technology can bring shoppers do not need to spend much time to visit shops to buy any things. They can choose any kinds of products from any online sellers individual online webstores conveniently at homes. Online technology excite busy consumers can make purchase decision easily as well as it can help online sellers sell any kinds of products from internet easily.

In behavioral economic view, technology can change human behavior to be improved, it can let human feels comfortable, more free time ro use, rapid making any decisions, such as apply smart phones to make share purchase or sale transaction decision, online shopping decision, even travelling any where decision in short time, when the traveller finds the most cheap hotel accommodation room price and air ticket price frm any travel agent online tourism webstore, then the potential travel customer can follow the online hotel accommodation price and air ticket price data to make decision when to buy the air ticket from the airline travel agent or make decision when to prebook which hotel accommodation room to go to the country to travel from online travel agent tourism webstores. So, technology can encourage global any country travelers to make anywhere to trvel rapidly. If the traveler can find the country's general hotel rooms and airline tickets prices had been decreasing more sightly. The traveler may make travel decision to choose the country to travel in short time, then he/she can prebook the country;s any hotel room and airline ticket to pay by visa fraom the country's any hotel and airline travel agent webstores., before one week, even one month or more easily. Hence, online technology can also encourage traveler individual frequent travel times to be increased, due to global travelers can find any hotel rooms and airline tickets prices from internet conveniently at homes. They do not need to spend time to visit any airline travel agent to enquire travel choice country's hotel rooms prices and airline ticket prices. They can compare global travel of countries choices ' all hotels rooms and airline agents air tickets prices to make prebook airline seat and hotel room decision before one week, one month even six months early.

On conclusion, online technology can encourage global travelers can make travelling any where and when traveling time desicions easily. It can excite tourism industry develops in long time. Also, such as electricity cars invention can encourage environment protection car owners do car purchase decision easily, because they can choose to drive electronic energy cars to replace oil energy cars in order to avoid air pollution occurs easily. So, electronic cars can increase electronic car purchasrs number, due to many of environmental protection attitude of car owners can choose to drive electricity cars to bring air cleans, even non -manual driving cars can encourage lazy driving and free time driving car owners to choose to buy non-manual (artificial intelligent) cars to drive , because they can spend much free time to read, listen music or do any matters in themselves cars, they do not need to drive cars, robotic (AI) auto driving machine is such one non-manual driver to help them to drive themselves cars confidently. So, non-manual driving cars can attract lazy and enjoying free time driving car owners to choose to buy to replace traditional manual cars to drive easily. Moreover, online share transaction can help any share investors to make share buying and selling decision in short time easily. When they can apply smart phones technological tool to carry on share buying and selling activities easily. They can observe any share rising or falling price suitation from smart phones in any where any any time easily. So, smart phone technology can help global any shareholders to make share purchase and sale transaction easily. So, technology can encourage human makes decision in short time rapidly.

How and why employees behaviors may influence economy development?

In behavioral economy view,I believe the country's any organizational employees behavior may bring indirect relationship to influence the country's long term economic development. I shall indicate past manufacture industry social development period to explain their relationship. For many countries' past business activities had belonged to manufacturing industry, such as US, UK past before 1980 year, it focused on steel manufacturing and steel manufacturing related machine products. So, US, Uk developed countries manufacturing industries may be past main country's economic income sources. I assume US , UK past had one million number different kinds of industries. They ought had about seven houndred thousand number organizational businesses were belonged to manufactured industry. They may include:

Steel manufacturing and steel related machine manufacturing, e.g. vehicle manufacturing, home appliances, e.g. washing machine, television, radio, refrigerate cooler, heater, air condition etc. different kinds of different kinds of steel -related manufacturing machine, they were manufactured from US, UK steel machine manufacturers. So, US, Uk the other three hundred thousand number industry may be general service industry, e.g. hotel service, restaurent, cinema, public transport service, tourism lesiure , wine bar, supermarket etc. different kinds of non-manufacturing industries business organizations were operated in UK, US past before 1980 year.

So, in UK, US developed countries industry development history, they ought have high percentage of businesses belonged to steel related manufacturing machine and steel products. Also, in the past before 1980 year, US, Uk business employers , they employed many workers are manufacturing workers. They needed to spend long time to work in factories. They were skillful workers, and they are trained to manufacturing cars, washing machine, television, heater, etc. even steel itself different kinds of steel related products to prepare to deliver to their shops to sell to US, Uk local or overseas clients.

So, I believe that past UK, US ought employ many employees, they belonged to skillful manufacturing workers, manufacture increasing steel machine or steel related machine number of products rapidly daily. So, if UK, US had had many of these manufacturing factories owned high skillful workers, then their manufacturing steel-related machine or steel both kinds of products number must be influenced to raise rapidly. Consequently, their steel machine manufacturing products would been exported to overseas or would been sold to local both markets , they may be influenced to raise sale number. They (these manufacturing workers) needed to be trained to know how to manufactur these different kinds of machine products in the efficient teams and they ought to be trained to raise their efficiencies in order to shorten time to manufacturing many kinds of steel related manufacturing machine or steel itself products rapidly. So , if their efficiencies and manufacturing performance was improved, these US, UK any one manufacturing worker and their teams ought achieve raising productivities significantly.

Hence, when past UK, US manufacturing industry development period, if these two countries' any manufacturing factories could have many manufacturing workers could be trained to be skillful and proficient manufacturing workers. Then, in past every day to these factories workers, they ought help their steel or steel related manufacturing employers to raise any kinds of machine or steel products number in every team. So, when past in the manufacturing industry development, US, UK could have many factories' manufacturing workers themselves steel or steel related machine products manufacturing skill could be trained to to improve to any kinds of these machine or steel manufacuring products quality as well as their products number could be influenced to raise by themselves skillful improvement significantly every day.

Then, what would be influenced to occur to past UK, US manufacturing industry period? In behavioral economic view, when these two manufacturing industry developed countries, such as UK, US , if they had many factories workers can be trained to improve their skill in order to achieve any kinds of steel or steel-related machine products quality could be improved as well as products manufacturing number could be also increased absolutely.

In consequence, past UK and US both countries ought increase themselves any kinds of steel and steel related machine products number to be supplied to themselves local shops to let local clients to choose any one kind of machine manufacturing products to buy easily as well as they could also export to supply overseas any countries to buy their different kinds of steel or steel related machine products to let overseas steel or steel related manufacturing machine product buyers, they can have many of these different kinds of these steel or steel-related different kinds of manufacturing machine from UK and UK these both countries easily to compare other countries.

On conclusion, I believe that past US, and UK macro manufacturing industry income GDP would increase significantly. So, they would have good economic growth performance because when many of these manufacturing workers themselves manufacturing effort could be improved. So, it explained when employees manufacturing abilities can influence economic growth indirectly.

Robots invention whether they can help organizations to raise efficiencies or inefficiencies?

In behavioral economic view, in any organizations, when the organization hopes its worker teams can raise efficiencies , the organization may choose to increase more workers number and/or it can provide training to improve these workets themselves skills in order to raise their efficiencies. For one warehouse example, when the warehouse increases many goods , they are needed to delivered these goods from the shelves to the delivering destination locations. If this warehouse supervisors feel these workers themselves goods delivery speeds are slow, which is possible due to this warehouse's workers number is not enough. So, this warehouse supervisor ought increase workers number in order to increase their goods delivery speed in order to deliver goods from the shelves to every indicated goods delivery destination in order to let any one lorry driver can transport the right kinds of goods and ensure the accurate goods number to transport to any one client home rapidly.

However, if this warehouse supervisor planed to buy several warehouse goods delivery robots to assist these warehouse workers to find the right kinds of goods from shelves and then deliver to the right destination location in the warehouse. So, these warehouse orkers can concentrate on counting the accurate goods number and ensuring the right kinds of goods in order to prepare to let lorry drivers to transport these goods to these goods of buyers themselvers homes rapidly. Consequently, in the first step, robots can concentrate on finding th right goods from shelves and delivers them to the right goods transportation of location destination. Then, in the second step, these warehouse workers can concentrate on counting the accurate goods number and ensuring the right kinds of goods in order to prepare to put them to the lorry. Consequently, when warehouse robots and warehouse workers can cooperate to work together, the most important, robots, can deal on finding the right kinds of goods and deal on delivering the accurate number of goods of job duty as well as these warehouse workers can only concentrte on counting the right kinds of goods number in order to avoid it has none any mistake of wrong kinds of goods and inaccurate goods of delivery number to be transported to the lorry and to deliver to any one buyer's home.

So, it seems that warehouse robots ought help any one warehouse worker to raise himself efficiency and avoid goods delivery of mistake occurrence easily as well as their help to warehouse workers that can let any one goods buyer feels their goods can be delivered to their homes rapidly. Moreover, warehouse robots can also help these warehouse workers to raise efficiencies because warehouse robots can help them to shorten goods delivery time between any one shelf and any one goods delivery destination of location in the warehuse because robots may help them to find the right kinds of goods from the right shelf in the short time. So, any one worker does not need to spend long time to seek anywhere is the right shelf location for the kind of goods when the kind of goods are needed to deliver to the buyer's home from lorry. Warehouse robots can help them to do this aspect of " finding the goods from the right shelf in short time job duty". So, any one warehouse worker only needed tospend less time to do the counting of any right kind of goods number and ensuring the right kind of goods job duty. Consequently, this warehouse 's any one worker, his any one kind of goods delivery time may be reduced, because robots' assistance and they may have more confidence to avoid mistake to deliver the wrong number of goods and/or the wrong kind of goods to any one goods buyer's home.

On conclusion, it seems that warehouse robots ought may help any one warehouse worker to raise efficiency for any one team in the warehouse as well as the warehouse any one supervisor does not need to spend much time to observe any one worker individual performance for " goods delivery job duty aspect" because their goods delivery job duty that had been replaced to do by these several warehouse robots. Robots can achieve the more accurate of right kinds of goods and the right number of goods delviery job performance to compare any one of human warehouse worker themselves right kinds of goods of delivery and right number of goods of delivery job performance. So, when robots can participate to cooperate with this warehouse's any one worker to do their goods of delivery job duty in this warehouse every day. Then, robots can raies any one of supervisor individual confidence in order to let they do not need to spend time to observe any one of worker individual whose goods of delivery job performane. They can concentrate on supervising any one worker whose goods transport to lorry in the final step in order to avoid to deliver wrong goods number and / or wrong kind of goods to any one goods buyer's home every day. Consequently, this warehouse's overall teams of their delviery of goods performance many be improved by robotss' participatin to goods of delivery task as well as this warehouse's oveall teams themselves efficiencies may be influenced to raise by robots' goods of delivery task participation.

Why social behavior may influence organizational strategy needs to be changed ?

Why any organizations need to know whether nowadays social behaivor how has been changing in order to implement the kind of the most right strategy to achieve the profit aim pursue in possible. I shall indicate nowadays ecommerce or online, customer shopping behavior to explain above question concerns they ought have close relationship between social behavior and organizational strategic choice or organizational behavioral changing need.

On nowadays ecommerce business, or online shopping model, this kind of shopping model in global many young and old age consumers like to apply internet tool to choose any country sellers website stores in order to stay at home to buy any kinds of products from themselves webstores in global societies.

In fact, online shopping model had been popular for long time above to twenty years. Most of global sellers will make decision to design themselves webstores in order to attract global many online buyers to choose to buy their products from themselves webstores. So, it seems that social consumers purchase behaviors had been changed to online shopping from internet invention.

Hence, social consumers purchase behavioral changes may influence any organizations' strategies need to be changed from visiting shops purchase strategy model to online purchase strategy model, if the seller still concentrate on concentrate on considerate how to design itelf , but neglects to considerate how to design itself webstore, e.g. how to design attract product photos to put on itself webstore, how to arrange sale price information location to be putted on webstore and visa card payment location on itself webstore in order to let any one online buyer can feel very easier to buy itself any kinds of products from itself webstore. Then, its potential online buyers will be influenced to increase number when they can find this online seller itself any kinds of products photes and every kinds of product sale price information and visa card payment channel locations easily from itself webstore.

So, it implies that nowadays any one seller ought need to design one webstore to let any one online overseas and domestic consumers can have chance to click itself webstore to choose any one kind of product to buy conveniently when he/she does not hope to leave him/her home to go to shop, because nowadays social shopping behaviors had been influenced to change when internet invention, them it gives another online purchase method to replace visiting shops purchase method to global any one buyer in nowadays societies.

So, if nowadays any one seller still concentrate on how to design itself shop display in order to put any kinds of product on shelf in order to let any one visiting shop customer to find the kind of product to buy, but it neglects to change to choose to pursue another new technological shopping method, such as webstore purchase method in order to implement effective strategy to design the most right webstore as well as in order to attract global overseas and local consumers to find itself webstore easily from website and find its any one kind of product phots and sale price and visa card payment button in order to choose to buy itself any kinds of products in the short time. Consequently I believe that the seller will lose many customers from overseas and local when its other same or similar product sellers choose to design themselves webstores in order to let global any one product buyer can buy themselves any one kind of product when they can pay visa card to buy their products from them webstores conveniently when they stay at home habitly. Then, the seller will lose many global potential customers in long time.

On conclusion, in behavioral economic view, any consumer behavioral social changing, which will influence any in order to avoid customers number loses significantly . In future time, organizations need to make rapid decision in order to implement the most reasonable and the most useful strategy in order to avoid global potential customers number reduces or lose them in long time. So, social behavioral changing environment ought influence any global organizations need to decide how to change themselves strategies in order to avoid customers loses significantly in future time.

How and why human behavior may influence economic growth or recession?

May ourselves daily behaviors influence our global societial continue economic growth or recession? Do they have cause and effect close relationship between human behaviors and global economic growth or recession? I shall apply behavioral economic theory to analyze and explain whether ourselves daily behaviors and our global societial economic growth or recession which have close cause and effect relationship as below:

Every country itself economic development must depend on any business activities, otherwise, any kinds of business activities must need ourselves business activities or behaviors in order to achieve any business activities as well as achieve the country's overall economic development in macro view. However, any country's overall business activites or behaviors which must depend on any kinds of individual businessmen, themselves employees daily working behavior or activity or performance in order to help them to attract or increase many clients number to acieve " earning profit" aim. So, it seems that any individual business, itself overall every department individual working behavior is one main factor to influence the company's overall business performance.

For agricultural fruit and meat food farming industry example, such as New Zealand is a farming main target industry country. It had had many New Zealanders were daily themselves own farming businesses for many years. Their farming businesses include growing fruit, sheep, cow, pig pork, meat etc. food sale business. If the New Zealand farmer owned a large size farming land, then he will choose either growing fruit or feeding sheeps, pigs, cows to be meat to to transport to New Zealand supermarkets to help them to sell to their farmers meet to New Zealanders in order to earn profit. Thus, if the New Zealand farmer owned large size of farming lands, then he needs to employ many farming employees (farming workers) to help him to carry on farming business daily tasks, e.g. picking up friuts, feeding pigs, cows, sheeps to eat food daily. These daily farming jobs are very important to influence this New Zealand farmer's meats or fruits sale number whether they can be easy or diffcult to sell in New Zealand supermarkets , if these farming workers can own encough farming knowledge or skill to know how to pick up fruits method and make judgement to know whether it is right time to pick up the kind of fruits from the trees , as well as know how feed this pigs, sheeps, cows to eat food in order to let they are better health. Consequently, their farming behaviors which can let these animals can provide the best taste and enough meat from these animals to let New Zealander to buy to eat from New Zealand any one supermarket. Even these New Zealand farming workers can know whether the kinds of fruits, e.g. oranges, apples, gapes etc. fruits whether they ought be picked up from the trees at the right time. Consequently, they can make judgement to decide to pick up any kinds of the best taste fruits to let any one New Zealander to buy to eat from any one supermarket in New Zealand. Otherwise, if they do not make judegement to know whether the kind of fruit ought not be picked up because they still need longer time to continue grow up to increase fruit size and better taste from the trees in order to let any one fruit buyer can feel better taste when they eat this kind of fruit later. If they can buy this kind of fruit to eat later, then this New Zealand farmer's his fruit buyers can buy the best taste of this kind of fruit to eat from an yone supermarket in New Zealand. Consequently, many New Zealand supermarkets will choose to buy any kinds of fruits from this farmer fruit supplier when they feel this farmer's fruits can provide more better taste fruits to compare other farmers' fruits.

Thus, due to New Zealand is one farming main income source country. It's any kinds of fruits and meats need to be export to overseas to sell , instead of local sale. It's GDP percent is very high to whole country 's overall income source. So, any one New Zealand farmer individual and any one farming worker individual working behavior will influence its economy whether it is influenced to grow or recession possible. Moreover, it also seems that farming workers' farming knowledge and skill will influence themselves farming daily activities to achieve the aim of the number of increase or decrease to any kinds of fruits whether they are better taste or the number of increase of decrease to any kinds of meats whether they are better taste to supply to any one New Zealand fruit or meat buyers to eat from any one New Zealand supermarket. So, it implies that any one New Zealand farming worker individual farming behavior may influence any kinds of fruits or any kinds of meat taste because they are transported to any one supermarket to sell in New Zealand.

Consequently, if New Zealans had many farmers can teach god farming knowledge and skill to let their any one farming workers know how to decide judgement to decide when it is right time to pick up any kinds of fruits from trees , or how to grow them on soil in order to let they can grow rapidly. Then, many different kinds of fruits can be provided to let any one New Zealanders can eat the best taste of fruits when their fruits are supplied to any one New Zealand supermarkets. Even, if they knew how to feed foods to pigs, cows, sheeps to eat daily. Then they can be more health and they can provide the best taste of meats to let any one New Zealanders can buy their meats from any one New Zealand supermarkets. Moreover, their fruits and meats can be transported to overseas to let any one country fruits or meats buyers can choose any kinds of New Zealand meats and fruits to buy to eat from themselves countries supermarkets. Then, many overseas fruit and meat buyers will perfer to choose New Zealand any kinds of fruits or meats to buy to compare other countries fruits or meats to buy when they go to any one local supermarkets.

On conclusion, it seems that New Zealand farming workers themselves farming behavior may influence their farming employers any kinds of fruits or meats sale number and income because their farming task behaviors must influence whether their fruits or meats taste are the better taste or worse taste to compare their other local farmers (the farmer competitors) whose fruits or meats taste. If tthe farmer's any one farming worker can be trained to learn how to know to feed animals skill and when is the most right time to pick up any kinds of fruits from trees or how to grow them on the soil methods. Due to these farming worker individual farming behavior may influence his different finds of fruits and meats sale number to be increase or decrease, so these any one New Zealand farmer must need to depend on any one farming worker whose farming working methods, if their farming working behaviors can be the best to influence any kinds of fruits to grow rapid or any kinds of pigs, cows, sheeps animals grow up rapidly , then their sale number may be increase significantly and their taste can be improved to let any New Zealand or overseas meat or fruit buyer to buy to eat to feel from any one New Zealand or overseas supermarkets, then New Zealand's agriculture industry must be influenced to increase. In the world, any one fruit or meat buyer must choose to buy New Zealand's fruit and meat to eat in prefer to compare other countries' fruits and meats. So, New Zealand's GDP may be influenced to raise from any one New Zealand farming worker individual farming working behaviors. It seems that New Zealand farmer fruit and meat sale number is depended on their eatting consumers demand more than their meat and fruit supply because if these NZ farmers can apply high technology method to grow good taste fruit or feed good taste meat to let global eatting customers to feel, their demand will increase, then NZ farmers will need to increase good taste fruit and good taste meat supply number to satisfy global meat and fruit eatting customer taste need.

Investing in office technology can bring what advantages

Why ought any kinds of businesses need to invest in technology to offices when businessmen began to do businesses? The reason is simple, such as

any offices need email to communicate to let different departments staffs can contact to do any tasks in short time. So, email can replace telephone calling communication channel between departments in offices. Moreover, for paper files, electronic files may replace to keep to save any office confident documents or general memos, letters, reports etc. documents. So, paper printing number may reduce. Even some businesses began to sell their products from online webstores to let customers to pat visa to buy their products from their webstores conveniently. Hence, computer technology is essential to nowadays any kinds of businesses offices.

The best are developed with the entire project-focused organization in mind. For example, a question on resourcing could involve looking a cariety of systems and files with no way to automatically generate the rught combination of data. Hence, any business offices ought need a single, centralised database which keeps accounting, project and even HR information and can integrate data when required.

ON the office investing in technology web-based system with mobile access benefit, due to investing globalization and pressure on fee rates means staff are in the office less

frequently than ever. A web-based system means data can be accessed from

PCs and networked laptops with no other software needed. So, instead of offices can apply laptops and intra-internet communication technological tool, which can also offer the option of a mobile applications suite which means personnel working on -site can enter timesheet and expense reports from laptops, even when not connected to the central data base. This helps minimise time delays, streamlining the billing process and improving cash flow. So, office mobile onlinesite technology may help thme to bring real-time , easy access benefits. For exmaple, if a staff is

still making decisions based on information that is seven or eight weeks old, the staff will be surprised by the power of having real-time information at the

staff's fingertips. At any time this will give the staff an accurate "snapshot" of the health of the staff's

project, enabling the staff to take preventive action if the problems arise before it is too late.

This visualisation ensures that all key stakeholders can identify project problems immediately they happen . It's also an ideal way for directors or other managers to

grab headline information before a short notice meeting, for example, all of office laptop, mobile intra-internet, onsite technology may help to ensure more targeted decisions and better project control. Hence, office technology may help any business offices to save more time deal urgent tasks daiuly. It means that office technology may help any offices to save much time in long term.

For some businesses office technology may help their businesses to manage on projects to achieve rapid finishing in short time, such as all projects of harbour construction business aspect, some projects may face complex to prolong time to finish. SO, defining a discipline as " complex project management assumes that one can find projects cause of complexity". Also, any the harbour business projects do not really exist. The term project is a contract used to describe a particular human activity. Hence, if the harbour construction company managers can let its all harbour construction managers to apply mobile onsite technology, intra-internet communication channel to do daily communication tasks in short time between their different construction teams. Then, these new harbour onsite mobile intra-internet communication technology ought help all onsite harbour construction managers can supervise all harbour onsite workers to construct all harbour construction projects in short time efficiently and effectively.

Sp, on-site mobile intra-internet communication technology may be future construction industry which a kind of essential onsite mobile intra-internet communication

technoogy.Moreover, on-site mobile intra-internet communication technology can bring future construction industry on time to save cost and construction quality

improvement benefits. Due to increasingly construction industry and clients demand more for less and this is in a traditionalty high risk industry. The problem of

construction and its relatively slow pace of change seem to stem from its competive building living demand role in providing building buyer value. With its attendant

professions, it is often too remote from the customers' experience of their buildings.

When if the construction company really knew how to add value for building clients? What if the construction firm could improve productivity among those using the building?

How much is that worth? What if the school could improve performance of students in shcools and the recovery of patients in hospitals? Such improvements represent much cost

benefits that could mean that the building pays for itself. However, nowadays building technology can bring these key benefical features to any construction companies, such as

value success are committed leadership providing the vision, suitable values and effective shared processes.

How office technology brings intelligent thinking to office staffs? Finally, I beleive that if the company can invest technology in office. It will bring intelligent

thinking to office staffs in order to improve efficient and performance, because investing in office technology , which is a way to reduce risk without

going over the top through effective use of the company networks. Why can office technology working environment can help staffs to bring intelligent thinking in order to

improve performance and raise efficiency?

The reason of office technology working environment can excite staffs their intelligent thining to be raise. What's lacking is a way of mitigating against these risks and doing so cost- effectively. Because more recently, a new stage has been reached where office staffs rely not only on their technical and business knowledge, but now have methodologies and tools so sophisticated that they can forward predict and control any office projects to finish before due date more easily.Hence, with good technical knowledge, sound business underatanding, a good way of methodologies, and training in the very latest software technology to hand, these are the not investing in office technology staffs, those who still find it impossible to deliver projects successfully more easily before any their office projects finishing due date. What needs to be addressed to change this situation?

The main factors critical to improve office staffs performance and improve efficiency, the non-investing in office technology working environment ought to

changed to invest technology to office working environment in order to excite staff individual working emotion to bring raising efficiency, even improve performance effectiveness.

ON conclusion, any offices need to invest technology to offices in order to bring " improving technical skill to staffs their working environment", because

they need to know that skill does not equate to competence , and there fore, a competence and therefore a competency based assessment is essential so that a

prospective office employee knowledge and understanding, attitude and skills can be evaluated. So, technological office can help managers to evaluate office employee

individual job skill more easily in order to make decision whether skill is high or low to let high skillful staffs can continue to be trained to work

in offices as well as fire the low skillful staffs. So, when the office can attempt to spend more money to invest to its office working environment, it means that the organization should be investing in training for permanent staffs in the scarce skills working markets. A small

investment in office technology can reap significant benefits further down the live, such as planning for skills scarcity on investing nowadays office technological working environment.